COUNTRIES IN THE NEWS

AFGHANISTAN

Kieran Walsh

Rourke

Publishing LLC

Vero Beach, Florida 32964

www.rourkepublishing.com

The country's flag is correct at the time of going to press.

PHOTO CREDITS:
Cover, © Philip Baird/www.anthroarcheart.org; pages 13, 15, 18 © Getty Images; all other images © Peter Langer Associated Media Group

Title page: Afghanis gather near the border between Afghanistan and Pakistan.

Editor: Frank Sloan

Cover and interior design by Nicola Stratford

Library of Congress Cataloging-in-Publication Data

Walsh, Kieran.
  Afghanistan / Kieran Walsh.
      v. cm. — (Countries in the news)
Includes bibliographical references and index.
Contents: Welcome to Afghanistan — The people — Life in Afghanistan —
School and sports — Food and holidays — The future — Fast facts —
The Muslim world.
  ISBN 1-58952-676-7 (hardcover)
  1. Afghanistan—Juvenile literature. [1. Afghanistan.] I. Title. II.
Series.

  DS351.5.W35 2003
  958.1—dc21
                                    2003005803

Printed in the USA

CG/CG

TABLE OF CONTENTS

WELCOME TO
AFGHANISTAN

Afghanistan is a large country in central Asia. It is located between Pakistan to the south and east and Iran to the west. At its widest point, the country is about 870 miles (1,400 kilometers) across. It is slightly smaller than the state of Texas.

Two natives meet in a store in Afghanistan to drink tea.

Afghanistan became a fully independent country in 1919. Before that, both Russia and Great Britain had controlled the land.

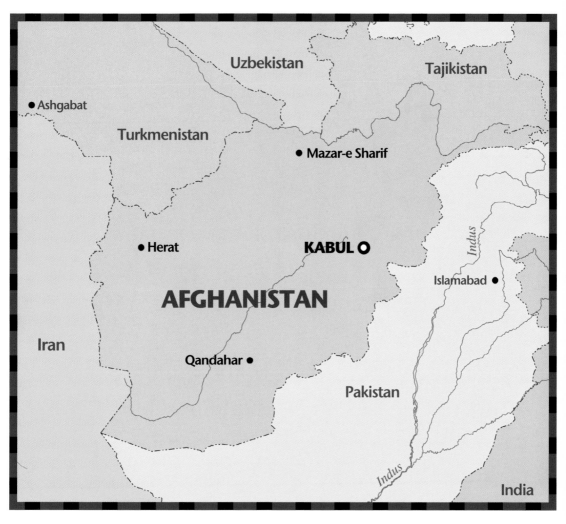

Until recently, Russia and Afghanistan were at war. Today the United States is the country most active in Afghanistan.

Afghanistan is **landlocked**, which means there are no large bodies of water touching it. Many people feel that because of this, Afghanistan has had little contact with other countries and is not as modern as it could be.

The name Afghanistan means "land of the Afghan." Afghanistan is a country of deserts, plains, and tall mountains. It also has many earthquakes.

The summers are hot. In the winter, there is often snow in the high mountains. One of the country's landmarks is the **Khyber Pass**, a deep **gorge**, near the border with Pakistan.

Kabul is the country's capital and largest city. But because of fighting in the last 20 years, much of Kabul lies in ruins.

A winding road in the Khyber Pass

THE PEOPLE

People who live in Afghanistan are known as Afghans. For many years, most of them were **nomads**, who wandered searching for food for their animals. Today, more and more Afghans want to settle in the growing towns and cities. Still, only about 20% of Afghans live in towns.

A man leads his camel.

A boy holds a tray of tea near the border with Pakistan.

Most Afghans are **Muslims**, which means they follow the teachings of **Islam**. About 85% are **Sunni** Muslims, and about 15% are **Shiite** Muslims. Until recently the country was run by a group known as the **Taliban**. These are devout Muslims who don't like change and look to the past rather than the future.

Afghans are made up of many different ethnic groups. Because of this, it is difficult to unify the groups into one whole.

Water is important to life in Afghanistan. Only 12% of the land there can be used for farming. Most of this land can be farmed only because of **irrigation**. About 70% of Afghans are farmers.

Only about 10% work in industry. Many of these people work in the carpet industry, where they make beautiful rugs by hand.

A carpet seller

LIFE IN
AFGHANISTAN

Families in Afghanistan are very close and often live together. Many of the men in the country have fought in Afghanistan's wars. As a result, in some homes women run the household and may even provide income. As in many Muslim countries, most women still cover their faces when they go outside.

Afghani women carry pots beside a railroad line.

An Afghani family is photographed inside a tent.

SCHOOL AND SPORTS

Education in Afghanistan is in terrible shape. Many buildings have been destroyed, and teachers are scarce. Foreign countries are bringing aid to schools in Afghanistan, and this may help the future of education. Very few women attend school at any level.

While many sports are popular, Afghanistan's national sport is **bazkashi**. In the game, riders on horseback try to bring an object into the scoring area. While it may sound easy, it is not. Horses are trained for five years before they can compete.

Only the best horses and riders can compete in the game of bazkashi.

FOOD AND HOLIDAYS

Most Afghans eat shish kebabs made of lamb, beef, and chicken. But Muslims do not eat any pork products. Rice is often served with the meat, and bread called **naan** usually accompanies the meal.

Ramadan is one of the most important Muslim holidays. It is the ninth month of the Islamic calendar. During this time, Muslims **fast** during the day and only eat lightly at night. When the month is over, Muslims celebrate **Id ul Fitr**. Then people visit each other and eat lots of good food.

Young Afghanis are shown in the prayer room of a mosque.

Afghani students sometimes attend classes outdoors. This is because of the shortage of schools and classrooms.

THE FUTURE

Afghanistan has recently been in the world's headlines. Afghans do not have easy lives. They have fought outside forces, but they have also fought among themselves. Much of the country has been destroyed, and many people have lost their lives.

The country has many problems: poor medical care, lack of good sanitation, and very little drinkable water. All these factors keep Afghans from living long lives.

! The economy of Afghanistan is one of the world's poorest. But, if money can be spent on human needs instead of on war weapons, Afghanistan might turn itself around. Only time will tell.

FAST FACTS

Area: 250,000 square miles
(647,450 square kilometers)

Borders: Pakistan, Turkmenistan, Tajikistan,
Uzbekistan, China

Population: 27,755,775
Monetary Unit: Afghani

Largest City: Kabul (2,734,000)
Government: Islamic state

Religion: 96% Muslims
Crops: nuts, wheat, fruits

Natural Resources: wool, fur pelts, mutton
Major Industries: textile, soap, furniture, shoes

THE MUSLIM WORLD

There are more than 1,200,000,000 Muslims in the world. Almost two thirds of them live in Asia and Africa. There are two major groups of Muslims: 16% of them are Shiites and 83% are known as Sunni.

Muslims follow the Islam religion. Muslims believe in God, who they know as Allah. The religion began around AD 610 when Muhammad became known as a prophet. He wrote down his teachings in a holy book called the Koran.

Muslims are required to pray five times a day. When they do so, they should pray facing Mecca, their holy city. They should also attempt to make a pilgrimage once in their lives to Mecca.

GLOSSARY

bazkashi (bazz KASH ee) — a traditional game played in Afghanistan

fast (FAST) — to go without food, usually for religious reasons

gorge (GORJ) — a narrow passage through land

Id ul Fitr (ID UHL FIT ur) — a holiday celebrated at the end of Ramadan

irrigation (ir uh GAY shun) — a system that provides water for growing crops

Islam (IZ lahm) — the religion followed by Muslims

Khyber Pass (KY buhr PASS) — a famous landmark in Afghanistan

landlocked (LAND LOCKD) — without access to any bodies of water

Muslims (MUZ lumz) — people who follow the religion of Islam

naan (NAHN) — bread eaten by Afghans

nomads (NOH madz) — wanderers who follow their livestock through desert regions

Ramadan (RAM uh DAN) — the ninth month of the Muslim year

Shiite (SHEE ITE) — a sect of Muslims, known for being liberal

Sunni (SOO NEE) — a sect of Muslims, basically conservative

Taliban (TAL uh BAN) — a group of Afghani Muslims, who are very conservative

FURTHER READING

Find out more about Afghanistan with these helpful books:

- Banting, Erinn. *Afghanistan: The People.* Crabtree, 2003.
- Italia, Bob. *Afghanistan.* Checkerboard Library, 2002.
- Corona, Laurel. *Afghanistan.* Lucent Books, 2002.
- Marchant, Kerena. *Muslim Festival Tales.* Raintree Steck Vaughn, 2001.

WEBSITES TO VISIT

- www.afghan-web.com/
- afghanistannews.net/

INDEX

About the Author

Kieran Walsh is a writer of children's nonfiction books, primarily on historical and social studies topics. A graduate of Manhattan College, in Riverdale, NY, his degree is in Communications. Walsh has been involved in the children's book field as editor, proofreader, and illustrator as well as author.

MERIDIAN MIDDLE SCHOOL
2195 Brandywyn Lane
Buffalo Grove, IL 60089